What you should know about Bible translations

by G. Christian Weiss
Director of Missions
Back to the Bible Broadcast

A
BACK TO THE BIBLE
PUBLICATION

10,000 printed to date—1978
(5-7528—10M—68)
ISBN 0-8474-1126-5

Printed in the United States of America

Foreword

What You Should Know About Bible Translations is a much overdue book. The controversy over translations has gone to such an extreme that some well-meaning people have been persuaded that unless one uses the King James Version, he is in danger of treading on liberal ground.

Although the controversy over translations is an especially heated one at this time, it is not something new. Actually, controversy over translations became so serious in the Middle Ages that a few translators were imprisoned, and some were even persecuted to death.

One of the key reasons for such controversy is the concern for an accurate translation that reflects the inerrancy of the Scriptures. Zeal for such a high view of the Bible is to be admired. The Back to the Bible Broadcast takes a strong stand on the inerrancy of the original writings of those God inspired to pen the Holy Scriptures.

Because the translation controversy has once more entered an almost belligerent stage, we believe it is important to be brought up to date on the history of the Bible. In particular, it is important to understand how it has come down to us in various translations. Translating the Scriptures into other languages dates back to the years before Christ, so there is much history to be considered.

To this theme G. Christian Weiss has given very careful study and has expertly set forth the facts of history, which helps to place the various translations in their proper perspective.

It is most interesting to note that there was heated controversy over the King James Version when it was first issued and that the process of accepting it was very slow. Some of our forefathers actually came to North America in a protest against this translation ordered by the King, seeking freedom to use whatever translation they desired.

I believe that Brother Weiss has done a masterful job in setting forth a technical subject in language that is easy to understand. I believe this book is required reading for the believer who wants a better understanding of how the Bible has been transmitted down to the present and of how God has guarded the purity of the Scriptures throughout the centuries.

The purpose of this book is not to add to the present controversy over translations—or even to engage in it, for that matter—but to clarify the issues involved and to help confused Christians to gain a better understanding of the whole picture.

I believe the information in this booklet will enlighten the reader and give him a greater appreciation for the Bible, God's written Word. My prayer is that God may bless it to this end.

—Theodore H. Epp

Contents

Chapter 1

When and How the Bible Was Written

Why are there so many different translations of the Scriptures? Why does a verse in one differ from the verse in another? Which translation is best? Why replace the King James Version with newer ones? Are the differences between the translations significant?

New interest in how the Bible has come down to us has been aroused lately because of the rapidly increasing number of modern translations, or versions, in the English language. Earnest Christians are raising questions about the accuracy of the new versions and the reason for them. Questions are being raised both audibly and in writing, in private and in public.

To answer the many questions being asked about the early manuscripts of the Scriptures and the worth of contemporary translations is no small task. A satisfactory treatment of the subject would require a sizable book, and such books are available on this important subject.

Many of those who are wrestling with questions about translations, however, do not have either the time or the background to read extensively on this subject in books that are often filled with technical terms. To put the facts into brief and clear language is no small challenge and one that is undertaken only with dependence on God and on the understanding of the reader.

The Writers God Used

It is the general and reasonable assumption that Moses was the earliest writer of the Scriptures. This means that parts of the Bible were written as early as around 1500 years before the time of Christ. The last book of the Bible, the Book of the Revelation, was written about A.D. 100. The obvious conclusion is that the Bible in its entirety was written over a period of some 16 centuries. This means that the latest portion was written nearly 1900 years ago.

Attention should be called to the fact that the Book of Job may have been written by another author than Moses and could possibly date back to 2500 B.C. This would mean that the Bible was written over a period of 26 centuries. But the previously mentioned 16 centuries is a conservative figure.

The writers God used to record the Scriptures were men of various walks of life, including kings, scholars, poets, judges, prophets, shepherds, fishermen and tax collectors. In inspiring the Scriptures to be written, God worked through these individuals in such a way that He did not destroy their personalities; thus, their writing reflected their station in life. Yet God worked through these men in such a way that the words they chose were precisely the words he wanted them to select.

The men God used to record the Scriptures did not write the Bible in English or in any of our

8

modern languages. The Old Testament was originally written in ancient Hebrew (a few portions in Aramaic), and the New Testament was written in Greek.

Hebrew was the language of the ancient Israelites, which explains why the Old Testament was written in it. Greek was the popular language of the world at the time of Christ, as well as during the time of the early church; hence, the books of the New Testament were written in that language. So the versions now available in western contemporary languages are obviously not the original Scriptures written by the inspired authors. Rather, these are only translations from existing manuscript copies of the originals.

Inspiration of the Scriptures

Although the writers God used to record the Scriptures were men from commonly known vocations of their day, they were not ordinary men nor did they write under ordinary impulse or circumstances. This is emphasized by a verse in the Bible that states: "All scripture is given by inspiration of God" (II Tim. 3:16). The literal Greek wording in this passage is, "All scripture is God-breathed." The Greek word for "breathed" is the same as the word for "spirit." Hence, it would be correct to render the expression, "All scripture is God-Spirited"; that is, all scripture was produced by the Spirit of God in the hearts and minds of the biblical writers.

Another Bible passage directly states: "No prophecy of the scripture is of any private interpretation. For the prophecy came not in old time by the will of man: but holy men of God spake as they were moved by the Holy Ghost" (II Pet. 1:20,21). The context of this statement indicates that the prophecy in question refers to the Scriptures. These verses reveal that no scripture came about by the prophet's own interpretation because prophecy never had its origin in the will of man. Rather, men spoke from God as they were carried along, or impelled, by the Holy Spirit.

The biblical authors did not write by their own impulsion or from their own minds and wills. They were inspired by God's Spirit, who Himself moved and directed them. This is what sets the Bible apart from all other books and all other human literature. The belief in the divine inspiration of the holy Scriptures constitutes the cornerstone and foundation of true Christianity.

Literary Forms

The original writings of the inspired authors were in various literary forms. Parts of the Bible were written as history. In the Old Testament, the historical books include the five books of Moses (also known as the "Pentateuch") and the 12 succeeding books. In the New Testament, the historical books are the four Gospels and the Book of the Acts.

A fair proportion of the Bible was originally written in the form of poetry. The poetic portions are the Books of Job, Psalms, Ecclesiastes and the Song of Solomon, as well as sizable portions of the books written by the Old Testament prophets.

A large portion of the Old Testament is prophetic in nature, and much of this prophecy was written in the form of public discourses, or sermons. The Old Testament books of prophecy include Isaiah through Malachi. Certain portions of the New Testament are prophetic also, such as Jesus' Olivet discourse, parts of the New Testament epistles and virtually the entire Book of the Revelation.

A considerable portion of the New Testament was written in letter form. These letters are commonly referred to as the "epistles." The word "epistle" is simply a transliteration of the Greek word into English. The word itself means "letter." Under divine inspiration, the New Testament apostles wrote letters to various churches and individuals. These portions of the Scriptures are in the form of ordinary letters of the times; that is, they begin with the name of the writer and his salutation and end with personal greetings. This basic pattern was followed in all the New Testament epistles. Remembering this helps one to better understand the highly personal nature of these scriptures.

How the Bible Was Preserved and Reproduced

The original manuscripts of the Scriptures, written by the inspired authors themselves, are no longer in existence. They have long since perished by decay or otherwise become nonexistent. This is understandable when one considers the long period of time that has elapsed since the original writings

11

were made and the nature of the materials the writers used.

Since we no longer possess the original manuscripts, the following questions might well be asked: How do we know that the translations we have today are essentially the same as the original manuscripts? How has the Bible come down to us through the many centuries of time? Is the Bible text we have today accurate and reliable as the very Word of God?

We need to keep in mind that the science of printing, although commonly known and extensively used today, was not invented until the early part of the 15th century. Thus, all copies of the Bible until that time were reproduced by hand. A handwritten copy of a document is what the word "manuscript" signifies.

As indicated previously, the oldest portions of the Bible were written at least 1500 years before the time of Christ. The first printed Bible did not come off the press until 1456. It was printed in the Latin language and is believed to be the first book ever printed by movable type. Comparing these dates reveals that for a period of about 3000 years the earliest books of the Bible were copied and preserved in the form of handwritten manuscripts. The parts of the Scriptures written latest were perpetuated in the same way for about 1500 years.

The first English translation of the Bible, made by John Wycliffe around 1380, was produced before printing had been invented, so every copy of that version had to be copied by hand. Yet many copies of the Wycliffe translation were made and widely circulated during Wycliffe's lifetime and in the years following his death.

12

Men and Materials Used in Copying Scriptures

Producing copies of the sacred Scriptures was not left to careless or incapable persons. This was especially true concerning the Old Testament. Long before the time of Christ, the Hebrews had a specially appointed guild of literary scholars who alone were entrusted with the work of copying and preserving the manuscripts of the Scriptures. These scholars were chosen with great care, and they were extremely conscious of the fact that they were dealing with the sacred Scriptures, the divine Word of God. They did their work with utmost care and meticulous fidelity, in the fear of the Lord.

After the time of Christ there was also a special literary guild charged by the Hebrew people with the care and reproduction of Bible manuscripts. These were called the "Masoretes." The Masoretes were deeply devoted to the Holy Scriptures and were entirely dedicated to their work. They used almost phenomenal exactness in making manuscripts of the holy text. When existing manuscripts became old and shabby, they were destroyed lest the text should become corrupted by any illegibility that could lead to errors or omissions in future copying of the text.

The writing materials used in producing Bible manuscripts were basically of two kinds. An early common material was a substance known as "papyrus." This was made from the inner fiber, or skin, of the papyrus plant. This fiber was cut into strips, which were placed side by side. A second layer of similar strips was pasted over the first at right angles. When pounded and smoothed, a material that was similar to heavy wrapping paper resulted.

The other and more durable material used was the tanned skins of animals, mainly goats and sheep. The earlier form of this material is known as "vellum" and was a rather thick leather; the later, thinner form is called "parchment."

With the exception of the tables of stone on which the Ten Commandments were originally written, all of the sacred Scriptures were originally written on papyrus and/or vellum. All early copies were produced on the same material. Because the leather substance was more durable than the papyrus, the oldest complete manuscripts now available are on this material, although many thousands of papyrus fragments have been discovered in various parts of the Middle East and Europe.

Originally, the manuscripts were in the form of scrolls and were read by rolling the section, or pages, from one spindle to the other. Later, however, the separate pages were bound in book form known as a "codex" (plural, codices). The ink used in writing was compounded of extremely durable substances, and because of this Bible manuscripts that date as early as 200 years before the time of Christ still exist. With the use of quill pens, permanent ink and permanent materials to write on, the manuscripts proved to be amazingly durable. As indicated, however, the original manuscripts of the Scriptures are no longer in existence.

Not as much specific information concerning the men who were charged with the reproduction and preservation of the New Testament manuscripts is available. But it is apparent that early in the history of the church there was a similar con-

14

cern for New Testament manuscripts as there had been for the Old Testament manuscripts. When books were accepted as being God's own word and revelation, extreme care was taken in their preservation, reproduction and circulation. Such care is historically documented.

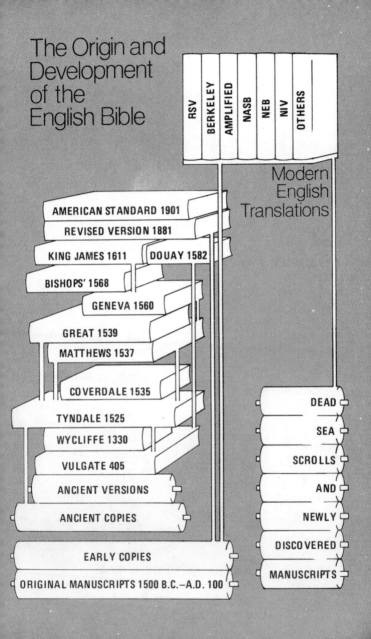

The Origin and Development of the English Bible

Modern English Translations

RSV
BERKELEY
AMPLIFIED
NASB
NEB
NIV
OTHERS

AMERICAN STANDARD 1901
REVISED VERSION 1881
KING JAMES 1611
DOUAY 1582
BISHOPS' 1568
GENEVA 1560
GREAT 1539
MATTHEWS 1537
COVERDALE 1535
TYNDALE 1525
WYCLIFFE 1330
VULGATE 405
ANCIENT VERSIONS
ANCIENT COPIES
EARLY COPIES
ORIGINAL MANUSCRIPTS 1500 B.C.–A.D. 100

DEAD
SEA
SCROLLS
AND
NEWLY
DISCOVERED
MANUSCRIPTS

Chapter 2

Manuscripts, Variations
and Early Translations

Without Hebrew and Greek manuscripts and the early translations, English versions of the Bible could not have been made. So it is important to understand the significance of the manuscripts, the variations found in those manuscripts and the development of early translations.

Hebrew Manuscripts

At the same time as the formation of the American colonies into an independent nation, Oxford College in England published a list of 615 then known Old Testament manuscripts. Approximately ten years later (1784-88) another list was published in Europe citing 731 manuscripts.

During the closing decade of the 19th century, some 10,000 fragments of Old Testament manuscripts were discovered in the attic of an ancient synagogue in Cairo. In 1947, the first of the famous Dead Sea Scrolls was discovered. These scrolls include thousands of Old Testament fragments representing every Old Testament book with the exception of Esther. The most remarkable of the Dead Sea Scrolls is the complete Book of Isaiah, dating back to around 200 B.C. The signifi-

19

cant thing about this manuscript is that it is almost identical to the ones of the Book of Isaiah already in possesion.

A renowned Jewish scholar, Moshe Goshen Gottstein, estimates that there are literally tens of thousands of Hebrew manuscript fragments in existence throughout the world. One collection in Leningrad, Russia, contains 1582 written on parchment, 725 on paper, plus at least 1200 additional fragments. The catalog published by the British Museum lists 161 complete Hebrew Old Testament manuscripts; and the Bodleian Library of Oxford lists an additional 146 Old Testament manuscripts. In addition, each of these contains a large number of fragments. It is estimated that there are more than 500 such manuscripts of the Old Testament in the United States.

Prior to the discovery of the Cairo Geniza manuscripts in 1890 and after and of the Dead Sea Scrolls in 1947 and after, the oldest Hebrew manuscripts available were copies made about 850. Therefore, when the King James Version of the Bible was translated, the earliest Hebrew manuscripts available to the translators were dated in the mid-ninth century. Since 1947, however, there have been Hebrew manuscripts available that date back to as early as the third century before Christ. The variations between these extremely old manuscripts and the later, previously known ones are amazingly slight. But it was the discovery of these older manuscripts that prompted the producing of the various new English translations, or versions, of the Scriptures.

The general concensus of scholars is that the oldest (earliest) copies of the Scriptures are naturally the most accurate and are likely to contain the fewest alterations and deviations from the original texts.

Greek Manuscripts

As with the Old Testament, the original, inspired New Testament manuscripts (also called "autographs") are no longer in existence. Since the originals were probably written on papyrus, they undoubtedly perished long ago. However, about 5000 New Testament manuscripts are in existence today, dating from approximately the third through the 13th centuries. Many are only fragments, but about 50 of these manuscripts contain the complete New Testament.

Ancient manuscripts of the Greek New Testament have been found in various parts of the Middle East—Egypt, Palestine, Mount Sinai and Asia Minor. Some have been found in lower Europe. Until about the middle of the 19th century, the oldest known manuscripts of the New Testament were dated around the middle of the eighth century after Christ. This means that until the mid-1800s, the oldest known copies of the New Testament Greek text were made some 650 years after the last book of the New Testament was written. Of the some 5000 Greek New Testament manuscripts now known, not less than 95 percent of them are dated from the eighth through the 13th centuries. But the other five percent—about 250 manuscripts—are from the second through the eighth centuries.

In the middle of the 19th century several very early and unusually significant manuscripts of the entire Bible were discovered. This new manuscript evidence led to the formation of a committee to produce a revised version of the English Bible. The Revised Version of the New Testament was published in 1881, and the complete Revised Version was published in 1885. The American Standard Version (ASV), which was basically the same version with slight alterations for American readers, appeared in 1901.

Variations of Readings

In the various manuscripts there are occasional differences of words or phrases. These are referred to as "variant readings." Of course the question arises, How significant are the known variations that appear in the different manuscripts?

Foes of the Bible have sometimes claimed that there are so many variations and contradictions in the different manuscripts that the text, as it exists today, is neither accurate nor reliable. Although the number of variant readings that are sometimes cited may seem disturbing at first, the variations actually occur in a relatively small percent of places in the Scriptures, and in no instance is the sense, or teaching, seriously affected. Some variations are only a matter of a different spelling of a word. But if such a word occurs 2000 times in a manuscript, unscrupulous critics might count this as 2000 separate variations.

Many of the variations in the different manuscripts involve only a different arrangement in the order of the same words in a given sentence, which does not affect the basic meaning of the sentence.

Scholars arrive at what they consider to be the

purest text (nearest to the original writing) by diligently comparing the many available manuscripts, generally regarding the older ones as more reliable. With the exception of a few dissident voices, capable and devoted scholars of the Scriptures believe that we have today a more accurate Greek text than was possible prior to the 19th century.

Principles of Evaluation

A principle that scholars normally follow as they evaluate various readings is to conclude that the more difficult, or harder to understand, reading is likely to be the correct one. The basis for this thinking is that as copyists produced manuscripts they might have had a tendency to clarify a difficult passage; thus, the difficult reading is normally preferred.

Another principle is that the shorter reading is normally the more accurate since a copyist might have had a tendency to add words to explain a passage if it appeared unclear to him.

Textual scholars also prefer the reading that seems to best fit the context, or passage, in which it is found. The reading that best fits the context is least likely to have been added as another reading.

Many of the old Bible manuscripts, and all of the most ancient ones, were written without spacing between sentences and even without spaces between words. Later, as the sentences and words were written with spaces between them, minor discrepancies occasionally appeared when a copyist was uncertain where to make the break between the letters. Even so, there are fewer discrepancies than might be supposed.

In addition, numerous variations in manuscripts are simply a matter of slightly different grammatical structures, which in no way change the basic meaning. A Greek copyist, for example, might correct a Hebraism (a Hebrew word or expression transliterated into Greek) because he considered it a violation of pure Greek grammar. Copyists sometimes substituted a Greek term in place of a Hebraism for the purpose of clearer and more understandable language.

Significance of Variations

The person who is unacquainted with the complex process of evaluating the manuscripts might think there is serious doubt about what was contained in the original writings. However, this is not the case. Two Cambridge University scholars, Dr. Brooke Foss Westcott and Dr. Fenton John Hort, who devoted many years of their lives to the study of Bible manuscripts and languages, estimated that only one-eighth of all the variations of textual readings had any weight at all, and only about one-sixteenth of these are more than mere trivialities. The conclusion is, therefore, that the Hebrew and Greek texts that have been derived from these various manuscripts can essentially be accepted as more than 98 percent pure, or almost exactly as originally written.

Dr. Philip Schaff, a renowned scholar and historian of the previous century, himself a theological liberal, calculated that of the multitude of variants sometimes cited, only 50 were of any significance. He also said that none of these affected the teaching or any basic doctrine of the Bible. The

Late A. T. Robertson, perhaps without an equal among biblical scholars in his generation, said there could be real concern over no more than a thousandth of the text. This would mean that the basic text of the Scripture is 99.9 percent free of significant variations or contradictions. When these few variations are compared to the number found in other ancient literary works, such as Homer's *Iliad* where a full five percent of the text is in serious doubt, it is safe to conclude that the Bible is the most accurately transmitted literary product of the ancient world.

It is important to understand that the words or phrases that are left out or added in reputable modern translations of the Bible are due to the different readings in the Hebrew and Greek manuscripts. Most of these variations that appear in English translations are relatively insignificant. Some later translations appear to be at variance with the time-honored King James Version, but it should be remembered that these variations are not based on the whims of the translators but on what they considered to be a more accurate Hebrew or Greek text. Of course, the precise wordings of the different translations vary, but in few instances does this seriously affect the sense, or meaning, of the Scriptures. This aspect will be considered in more detail under the discussion of Bible translations.

Ancient Translations

As already mentioned, the Old Testament was originally written in Hebrew and the New Testament in Greek. As these languages receded into limited use or almost complete disuse, translations in the current and more widely used languages were understandably needed and desired.

When the Hebrew language was replaced by Greek because of the widespread influence of the great Greek Empire, a translation of the Old Testament into the Greek language was desired. Such a translation was produced by Jewish scholars about 200 years before the time of Christ. Because the translation was presumed to have been made by a company of exactly 70 scholars, it was commonly called the "Septuagint," a Latin word meaning 70. This was the translation of the Bible used by the Jewish people for several centuries. It was probably the translation used by Jesus and His disciples, as well as the early church.

Although Greek remained the chief language of Christianity for two or three centuries after Christ, the powerful and expansive influence of the Roman Empire brought with it the widespread use and popularity of the Latin language. This created the need to have the Scriptures available in Latin. The earliest Latin version, with the Old Testament translation based on the Greek Septuagint, was made in Africa and was transcribed and distributed in various sectors of the Empire. Several revisions of that Latin translation were later made in order to delete provincialisms and other recognized defects in the African version. The most important of these revisions was done in Italy in the latter part of the third century by the eminent scholar, Jerome.

The differences and imperfections of the Latin copies led Jerome, on the urging of the Bishop of Rome, Damasus, to produce an entirely new translation with the Old Testament translated directly from the Hebrew manuscripts. This translation, known as the "Vulgate," became the official version appointed for use in the churches and was considered the authorized Bible of the Roman Church.

Jerome spent the greater part of 24 years doing his work and completed it in 405. The Vulgate is still considered by the Roman Catholic Church to be the official Catholic version of the Bible. Some 8000 manuscripts of the Vulgate are now known to exist, which indicates that the Vulgate version of the Bible was the most frequently copied book of all ancient literature.

Syriac, a language closely related to the Aramaic spoken during the time of Christ, was the language of the countries neighboring Palestine. Christian converts and churches in these countries wanted to have the Scriptures in their mother tongue, perhaps as early as, or even before, the first Old Latin Version appeared in North Africa. Thus, the "Old Syriac Version" was produced around the end of the second century.

The Old Syriac Version survives in two manuscripts of the Gospels discovered in Egypt in 1842 and at Mount Sinai in 1892. These two manuscript portions date back to the fourth and fifth centuries. However, the main Syriac Version is known as the "Peshitta," or "Peshitto," which means "simple." The Peshitta contains all the books of the Bible except II Peter, II and III John, Jude and Revelation. The Old Testament was evidently translated directly from Hebrew manuscripts and the New Testament from Greek manuscripts.

Other ancient translations produced from the middle of the fourth century and after include

Ethiopic, Egyptian Coptic, Gothic, Armenian and—in the ninth century—the Slavonic Version. At about the same time Arabic and Persian translations were made. These were followed later by translations of the Bible into German, French, Spanish, Italian, English and other languages. As of 1976, at least portions of the Bible are being circulated and printed in 1550 languages, which makes the Bible the world's most widely translated book.

The Basis of Bible Translations

From what languages and manuscripts were the various translations made? The answer to this question is a complex one, but it is vitally important. The early Bible translations were made from the Hebrew and Greek languages, based on the manuscripts available to the translators at the time they worked. But as time passed, the Hebrew language receded into disuse and finally became a "dead" language. It was replaced, as mentioned previously, by the Greek language, which was practically a universal language during the time of Christ.

During the first centuries of the Christian era, virtually all Bible translations and Bible literature were based on the Greek language. It was the original language of the New Testament, and the Septuagint (Greek translation of the Old Testament) had largely replaced the use of the Hebrew Scriptures.

Later, the Latin gradually replaced the Greek language and became the official language used in churches. Beginning with the fourth and fifth centuries and continuing to the 16th century, Latin was the chief language of Bible translations as well as other Christian literature and liturgy. It persisted even into the 20th century as the liturgical language of the Roman Catholic Church.

The Renaissance, which came into full bloom in the 15th and 16th centuries, brought a revival of classical learning and caused many scholars and intellectuals to turn back to the Greek language and literature. The Renaissance also gave rise to an attitude which strongly opposed restricted knowledge. This was another reason why churchmen suddenly became interested in going back to the original languages of the Bible rather than studying the Scriptures from the restrictions of a translation.

As early as 1502 Cardinal Ximenes of Toledo, Spain, began the significant work of preparing a Greek edition of the Bible. His plan was to produce an Old Testament with the Hebrew, Latin and Greek in parallel columns, and the New Testament in Latin and Greek only. Because of its use of many tongues, or languages, it was called a "polyglot." The Pope's approval was given in the year 1520, but the Cardinal's version was not actually made available until 1522. It became known as the "Complutensian Polyglot" because of the city in which it was produced. Although this was the first Greek edition of the New Testament to be put into print, it was not the first to be published and actually made available to readers.

Erasmus' Greek Edition

When a Swiss printer named Froben heard of Cardinal Ximenes' anticipated polyglot edition of the Bible, he went hastily to a Dutch scholar

29

named Desiderius Erasmus and urged him to prepare an edition of the Greek New Testament as quickly as he could. Froben's intent was to publish a Greek edition of the New Testament before Cardinal Ximenes was able to do so.

Erasmus was a widely known and influential scholar and produced a number of satirical and critical books written in his customary language, Latin. Although he was an ordained priest of the Roman Catholic Church and continued in that faith until his death, he was more of a humanist than he was a cleric. A humanist is one who believes in the goodness of man and thinks man can achieve self-realization through reason. Erasmus shunned the theological warfare of his time and would not support Martin Luther in the Reformation. This was a great disappointment to Luther since Erasmus had openly criticized the weaknesses of the Roman Church both in the pulpit and in the pew. Erasmus' failure to support Luther brought him stout opposition from Luther.

Erasmus' literary works combined vast learning with a keen and often malicious humor. It was said of Erasmus: "Whatever his individual talents, he was certainly the broadest of the humanists" (*Columbia Encyclopedia*, p. 627).

When Erasmus was approached by Froben about producing an edition of a Greek New Testament, he agreed to do so. Erasmus worked rapidly, beginning his work in September of 1515, and the following March his Greek New Testament was published. During the succeeding seven or eight years, however, four other editions of Erasmus' Greek New Testament were published, and minor changes and corrections were made in the text of each one.

Manuscripts Used by Erasmus

Although numerous Greek manuscripts were known and available at the time of Erasmus, none of them dated earlier than about the mid-eighth century. The one exception was the important manuscript known as Codex B, dated from the fourth century. It contained the entire Bible, although some parts of both testaments were missing. This famous manuscript was placed in the Vatican library in Rome about 1481, but it was not available for scrutiny or study by research scholars because the library authorities were reluctant to permit access to it. Therefore, Erasmus could not refer to Codex B.

Because of the haste with which Erasmus compiled his Greek text he utilized only a limited number of the available manuscripts, not more than six. In the later editions of his Greek New Testament, he consulted a few additional manuscripts, but the changes he made were comparatively minor.

All of the manuscripts that Erasmus had access to were those known as "The Byzantines"; that is, they came from the eastern (Greek Orthodox) branch of the church whose patriarch resided in Constantinople, originally known as Byzantium. The only non-Byzantine manuscript available to Erasmus was one known as Codex 1, although Erasmus apparently did not rely heavily on it.

It is noteworthy that a printer, not a biblical scholar, requested Erasmus to compile a Greek text from the various available manuscripts. The invention of printing, as well as the revival of learning which took place during the Renaissance, turned attention back to the Greek text of the Scriptures. Once printing became an established industry, it was quite natural that the Holy Scriptures in the original languages would be published and distributed widely, and that the original languages, rather than the previously accepted standard, the Latin Vulgate, would become the basis for future translations. Printing revolutionized the whole world of scholarship and literacy; thus, it had a profound effect on Bible publication and circulation.

Other Greek Editions

About a decade after the death of Erasmus, a man by the name of Robert Stephanus published four editions of the Greek New Testament. He used the text produced by Erasmus, Ximenes' Complutensian Polyglot, and compared about 15 Greek manuscripts. Stephanus belonged to a family of printers who lived first in Paris and later in Geneva. In his fourth edition, published in 1551, Stephanus introduced the verse divisions and numerations that are still in use today. Chapter divisions had been introduced by Stephen Langton, Archbishop of Canterbury, in the 13th century.

Between the years 1565 and 1604 Theodore Beza, an able Protestant scholar, published nine editions of the Greek New Testament. These editions were slightly revised but essentially the same as those of Erasmus and Stephanus. Beza's wide reputation helped to promote and set the form of a permanent printed Greek text. Shortly thereafter, between 1624 and 1678, two Dutch publishers in Holland, the Elzevir brothers, published several editions of the Greek New Testament based mainly on the texts of Beza and Stephanus.

The preface of the Elzevir brothers' second edition was written in Latin. The preface told the reader he had the "text [textum] now received [receptum] by all." Thus, the Greek text became known as the "Textus Receptus." These words are still applied to the standardized Greek text of the time of the Elzevirs.

It is important to bear in mind that the words "Textus Receptus" do not signify any authoritarian endorsement of a particular Greek text, as seems to be implied by some people today. Rather, these words came into use in quite an incidental way because of the Dutch publishers' introduction to the second edition of their Greek text.

Chapter 3

The Development
of English Translations

The growth of English translations of the Bible is an involved and intriguing study in itself. It is unfortunate that so few are familiar with the story.

The Bible was first brought to the British Isles in an early Latin version by the Roman conquerors and Roman emissaries. The last Roman soldiers officially left Britain in 410, and almost nothing is known about the experience of Christians in England during the following 200 years. However, monasteries were springing up throughout Ireland, and by 600 the study of sound literature was pursued with a thoroughness and intensity unknown elsewhere in Europe at that time. But there is no trace found of a vernacular translation (a translation in the common language) during that period.

A missionary by the name of Augustine (not to be confused with the earlier Augustine of North Africa), along with 40 monks, was sent to England by Pope Gregory the Great sometime in the sixth century. Canterbury Cathedral was founded during that century, and Augustine became its first archbishop.

In the following years, certainly as early as 700, various Anglo-Saxon translations were made of some portions of the Scriptures. The Venerable

Bede translated parts of the Bible, including the Gospel of John, as early as 735. King Alfred prefixed to his "Laws" a version of the Ten Commandments, and he also undertook to translate the Psalms, although he died before completing the work. Near the end of the tenth century, Aelfric, "The Grammarian," translated the Pentateuch and some of the historical books in Saxon. However, none of these translations were preserved, and their existence is known only as a matter of historical record.

John Wycliffe's Translation

The first great Bible translator of Britain was John Wycliffe, who completed an English translation from the Latin Vulgate about 1382. Following his death, Wycliffe's translation was revised by his devoted fellow laborer, John Purvey. Since this was before the time of printing, all copies of Wycliffe's translation were produced by hand. Yet for 150 years this was the only complete English translation in use.

Wycliffe's work was regarded with grave suspicion when it appeared, and a bill was introduced into the House of Lords to suppress it, although the bill was not passed at first. In 1408, however, the Convocation of the Province of Canterbury at Oxford resolved that no one should translate any text of scripture into English and that no such translation should be read publicly or privately until approved by ecclesiastical authority, on the pain of excommunication. This edict led to great persecution, but in spite of this there is reason to believe that many manuscripts of Wycliffe's translation were circulated extensively throughout England.

William Tyndale's Translation

After the death of Wycliffe, printing was invented, and in 1456 the first printed Bible (the Latin Vulgate text) came off Gutenberg's press in Germany. Bible manuscripts soon ceased to be handcopied. The next English translation of the Scriptures, produced in part by William Tyndale, was circulated in printed form, making copies available for the common man.

There was still strong opposition in Tyndale's time to publishing the Bible in the "vulgare tonge" of the English people. This opposition came from both the King of England (Henry VIII) and the clergy. In 1530, prior to his break with the Roman pope, King Henry issued a proclamation that the translation and circulation of the Scriptures in the common language of the people be forbidden, affirming that the people must " 'haue the holy scripture expouned to them, by preachers in their sermons, accordynge as it hath ben of olde tyme ... that the same bokes [Tyndale's] and all other bokes of heresy, ... be clerely extermynated and exiled out of this realme of Englande for ever.' " (*Wycliffe Bible Encyclopedia*, Vol. 1, p. 237).

William Tyndale said to one of his opponents, " 'I defy the Pope and all his laws; if God spare my life, ere many years I will cause a boy that driveth the plow shall know more of the Scriptures than thou dost' " (*Wycliffe Bible Encyclopedia*, Vol. 1, p. 236). Tyndale spent a good portion of his life in exile, and his translation of the Bible was printed

37

outside of Britain, at Hamburg, Worms and Cologne. With great intensity, the authorities attempted to suppress all the efforts of Tyndale and his group to put the Bible in the hands of the people in a language which they understood. There was a systematic, official effort to confiscate and destroy all copies of Tyndale's English translation of the Bible.

Tyndale himself was finally betrayed by a supposed friend and was martyred by strangulation at a stake, and his body was burned. He probably never saw a completed English translation that was the result of his own labors, but many copies of the New Testament had been circulated throughout the country by the time of his death. In the years immediately following his death, the Bible was widely circulated in England, although the Bishop of London and his assistants took great pains to buy up and burn all the copies they could.

The question might be asked, Why was Wycliffe's translation not sufficient? Why was it not printed and circulated rather than a new translation produced by Tyndale? There are two important answers to this question. First, Wycliffe's translation was based exclusively on the Vulgate. But Tyndale felt the necessity of a translation made directly from the Greek text (based on the earlier efforts of Erasmus), although he did consult the Vulgate and Luther's German version. Second, during those times the English language was in a state of development and flux, so that between the time of Wycliffe and Tyndale great changes had already taken place in the language, making Wycliffe's translation obsolete in many ways.

Miles Coverdale's Translation

Just prior to Tyndale's martyrdom, his close friend and fellow laborer, Miles Coverdale, produced an English translation of the Bible made from the German and Latin but also using Tyndale's work as a basis. This was, in fact, the first complete printed version of the Bible in English. By this time, Henry VIII had broken with the king of France and the pope of Rome. So in contrast to the experience of Tyndale, Coverdale did his work with the apparent approval of the king and under the patronage of Thomas Cromwell, adviser to King Henry VIII of England.

Two years after Coverdale's translation appeared, John Rogers, who had assisted Tyndale in his work, reprinted an edition based mainly on the Tyndale and Coverdale versions but also bearing traces of considerable and careful revision. This translation was " 'set forth with the King's most gracious license' " (*Wycliffe Bible Encyclopedia*, Vol. 1, p. 237). It was a significant improvement over the Coverdale Bible of 1535 and was published under the assumed name of Thomas Matthew; hence, it is commonly called "Matthew's Bible."

The Great Bible

The version known as "The Great Bible" appeared in 1539, two years after the publication of Matthew's Bible. The Great Bible was actually Coverdale's translation, revised by the translator himself under the public sanction and with the aid of Cromwell. Archbishop Cranmer wrote a preface to this version, and because of this it is sometimes referred to as "Cranmer's Bible."

Authorized copies of The Great Bible were placed in every church with the sanction of King Edward VI, who issued a proclamation for the Bible to be placed in the churches and made available for the people to read. To assure that the Bibles remained available to the public, they were often chained to a table. King Edward's decree read in part: " 'It was ordenyed and commaunded . . . that in al and synguler paryshe churches, there shuld be prouyded by a certen day nowe expyred, at the costes of the curates and paryshioners, Bybles conteynynge the olde and newe Testament, in the Englyshe tounge, to be fyxed and set vp openlye in euery of the sayd paryshe churches' " (*Wycliffe Bible Encyclopedia*, Vol. 1, p. 237).

The Geneva Bible

Following The Great Bible, other translations were printed in English, including another significant version known as the "Geneva Bible." This name was given to it because it was translated by Christian refugees who fled Britain during the reign of Queen Mary and produced the translation while living in Geneva, Switzerland. This version contained marginal expository annotations, both doctrinal and practical, some of which were highly controversial at that time.

The Geneva Bible was the first English translation to be printed in a handy size with numbered verse divisions, based on the plan originally employed by Robert Stephanus in his Greek New Testament of 1551. The Geneva Bible was also the first English translation printed in Roman type instead of in black letters, or the so-called Old English type. This was undoubtedly the most accurate English version available at that time and was the translation used by Shakespeare, John Bunyan and Oliver Cromwell. It was also fervently studied by the Puritans and brought to American on the *Mayflower*.

The *Mayflower* Pilgrims apparently had a strong aversion toward the King James Version and frowned on permitting its presence in the early colonies. Actually, the Geneva Bible—designated as "the People's Book"—held preeminence among the English versions for at least 75 years. Ultimately, however, along with all the other previous versions, it was displaced by the King James Version.

The Bishops' Bible and the Douay Version

In 1568 a revision of the existing English translations appeared. It was the work of Archbishop Parker, who had the help of various bishops and scholars. The work was published under the authority and sanction of Queen Elizabeth. Known as "The Bishops' Bible," this revision contained short annotations, and the text was divided into verses like the Geneva Bible, a pattern still followed in our contemporary translations.

The Bishops' Bible continued in common use in the churches and by the clergy for at least 40 years, although the Geneva Bible was the most universally read in private and was also frequently found in the churches. The Bishops' Bible was widely used until the middle of the 17th century;

that is, for nearly 50 years after the King James Version was published.

The first English Roman Catholic version was produced in the 16th century by the Divines of the English College at Douay in Flanders, from which it derived its name, "Douay Version." The New Testament appeared at Rheims in 1582 and the Old Testament at Douay in 1610, one year before the Protestant King James Version was published.

The "Authorized Version"

In January, 1604, King James I called for a conference at Hampton Court to consider an official revision of the English version of the Bible. For this purpose, the king appointed 54 men of outstanding learning and ability. Actually, 47 undertook the work, which was completed in four years, 1607-1611.

The translators were divided into six groups: three groups to work on the translation of the Old Testament, two groups to work on the New Testament, and one group to work on the Apocrypha. The result of this diligent translation work was known as the King James Version. All early editions of the King James Version included the Apocrypha in a separate appendix at the close of the Old Testament.

This time-honored version of the Holy Scriptures has held prominence longer than any other English translation. It is commonly known as the "Authorized Version" because the project was undertaken by a specific order from King James I and with his obvious sanction. The translators dedicated their version to the king. However, no direct evidence is found of any official English authorization, either civil or ecclesiastical.

King James I was the son of Mary, Queen of Scots. When Mary was forced to abdicate her throne, he became James VI of Scotland. Later, being in the royal line and with his eye on the British throne, he allied himself with England's Queen Elizabeth. This caused a break with his mother's party, and history testifies that he accepted her execution in 1587 with unperturbed calmness. The king himself was strongly anti-Puritan, but in order to conciliate the Puritan leaders, he presided over the Hampton Court Conference in 1604, at which the Puritans demanded recognized status in the Church of England.

At this conference the move was launched to produce a revision of the Bible which would be a new English translation. Several translations were in use at the time, and it was felt that so many translations created confusion. Also, there was certain dissatisfaction with existing versions. It is interesting that the situation at that time almost precisely resembles the present situation in the English-speaking world.

Historically, the reign of King James was noted for its inconsistent political policies, tyranny against personal foes, and the extravagance and looseness of the royal court. He insisted on the concept of the divine right of kings and did not give proper recognition to the parliament.

In 1611, the very year the Bible version of his sanction was published, he arbitrarily dissolved the parliament, which produced violent reactions. In fact, it was the arbitrary policies of King James that finally led to the Puritan revolution that broke out about the time of his death. Despite his dubious reputation as a monarch, however, the memory of King James I is revered among Christians because of the version of the Bible bearing his name. And the character of his regime does not alter the fact that the 54 scholars and churchmen he appointed did an amazing work in producing the most historically honored of all English translations.

Opposition to the King James Version

But as was the case with most previous English versions—and still is true today concerning almost all new Bible translations—the King James Version met with considerable opposition at first. This opposition did not take the translators by surprise. Their words in the preface indicate that they clearly anticipated opposition. They wrote: "Things of this quality have ever been subjected to the censures of illmeaning and discontented persons" ("The Epistle Dedicatory"). They anxiously desired that their work receive the king's approval, indicating that his acceptance of their labors "shall more honour and encourage us, than all the calumniations and hard interpretations of other men shall dismay us" ("The Epistle Dedicatory"). Then follows this significant statement: "So that if, on the one side, we shall be traduced by Popish Persons at home or abroad, who therefore will malign us, because we are poor instruments to make God's holy Truth to be yet more and more known unto the people, . . . or if, on the other side, we shall be maligned by selfconceited Brethren, who run their own ways, and give liking unto nothing, but what is framed by themselves, and hammered on their anvil; we may rest secure, supported within by the truth and innocency of a good conscience, having walked the ways of simplicity and integrity, as before the Lord" ("The Epistle Dedicatory").

It is wholesome and well that there are questions about any new translation of the Scriptures. This fact, in itself, indicates the sacred jealousy with which Christians regard the Holy Scriptures. But even though the King James Version met with opposition when it was first published and competed in popularity for a number of years with The Great Bible, the Geneva Bible and the Bishops' Bible, no other version achieved the popularity and historical longevity of the King James Version.

Because of its overall faithfulness in translation and its signally beautiful language, the King James Version at length prevailed by general consent over the previous English versions. For well over 300 years it was the most popular version of the English-speaking world. Even at present, 365 years after its publication, this version of the Bible still holds highest place among English-speaking Christians, in spite of the many modern English versions now in use.

From the standpoint of its literary worth alone, the King James Version stands out as the finest example of Elizabethan English in print. Although at first not welcomed in the American colonies, throughout the years of the United States' history, the King James Version has been a basic element in American life.

Chapter 4

Why Modern Versions?

Because of the proliferation of modern versions
of the Bible, confusion exists in the minds of many
Christians. When visiting churches or listening to
speakers, questions arise, such as: Which version
will the minister be using? Which version will the
Sunday school teacher use? Which version should
we and our children use in memorizing verses?
These are all common and valid questions raised by
those who are genuinely concerned about the rapid
increase of English translations.

But in spite of the problems, the Christian
must not close his mind to new translations. It is
good to ask, Why these modern versions? But we
should also ask, Why the *previous* versions?

Remember that there were seven great English
versions of the Bible prior to the appearance of the
King James Version. It is also significant to realize
that there have been several revisions of the King
James Version since its first publication. If the
average English-speaking person today saw the
King James Version as it was first published, he
would scarcely be able to read it.

It is important to realize that if it had not been
for the various English versions, the quality of the
King James Version would never have been
achieved. Each previous version was an improvement over the preceding ones, and the King James

47

Version was based on them. This was readily acknowledged by the translators, who stated on the front page of the King James Version that their work was "with the former translations diligently compared and revised." Although they were accomplished Hebrew and Greek scholars and translated from the original languages, they meticulously referred to previous versions and revised their own renderings in the light of them.

Why was the King James Version produced? It was to obtain a better translation. This is also the expressed reason why most of the translations are produced today.

Motives Behind Translations

With few exceptions, if any, translations of the Bible have not been made with the purpose of deliberately attempting to mutilate and corrupt it. Also, few translations have been made with the distinct motive of supporting a particular theological bias. A literary work such as a translation of the Bible is far too open to the public's scrutiny and criticism to allow petty motivation.

Two outstanding exceptions regarding theologically motivated translations are the New World Translation of the Jehovah's Witnesses and the so-called Inspired Version of the Mormon Church. But apart from these, almost all of the English versions of the Bible were produced by scholars of high integrity. Naturally, the theological convictions of any scholar have a tendency to affect his literary work, but most translations of the Bible were not deliberately made to support a particular theological or sectarian bias.

48

It is also important to remember that the majority of English versions have not been made by a single person or by those of one particular denomination. Although some popular versions are chiefly the work of an individual scholar, these individuals *NOTE* have generally been theologically sound. Translations produced by a single individual, however, are more likely to be deficient than those produced by a group of recognized scholars, especially if the group represents the work of several religious bodies.

As indicated previously, it is wholesome that each translation of the Bible is subjected to careful evaluation and even skepticism, but it is tragic that some Christians look upon each new translation as an attempt by its translators to corrupt or destroy God's Holy Word. Although all translations are imperfect and defective to some degree, it is wrong to condemn the motives of the scholars involved in their production. In most instances, the motives of the scholars are beyond reproach, regardless of the merit of the translations they produce.

The same kind of criticism being brought against modern English translations of the Scripture was also brought against the King James Version when it first appeared, and these criticisms dogged it for a good many years. When the English Revised Version (1881-1885) and the American Standard Version (1901) appeared, they also came under strong attack. However, within a quarter of a century they were regarded as probably the most accurate English translations of the Bible produced up to that time.

In fact, when the English Revised Version first appeared, the spiritual giant and prince of preach-

49

ers, Charles Haddon Spurgeon, expressed deep respect for its faithfulness of translation, although he disliked the English it employed. For years, the American Standard Version was the most recommended and commonly used version in the majority of fundamental Bible institutes and evangelical seminaries in the United States.

REASONS —

Language Considerations

On the positive side, several reasons prompted the producing of the later and more contemporary versions of the Scriptures. One of these reasons was to modernize and clarify the language of the Bible to make it more understandable to the people of this generation. It was a basic desire to have God's unchanging Word in clear language of current usage.

It is highly significant that when the New Testament was recorded by the divinely inspired authors, it was not in the classical Greek of the period but in the common language of the masses. It is known as *koine* Greek, which means "common." This indicates that God wants His Word in the most understandable language possible.

Today, when missionaries undertake the translation of the Scriptures into the language of the people among whom they are laboring, it is always their aim to use the most understandable language in their translation work. This same desire motivated Martin Luther to translate the Bible into the spoken language of the German people. His translation, like the King James Version, has stood the test of time because it was the language the German people understood and spoke.

The English language is an outgrowth of several languages and has undergone many changes through the centuries. This was one of the main reasons why Wycliffe's English translation had to be replaced 150 years later by the work of William Tyndale. A contemporary Englishman or American would scarcely be able to follow Wycliffe's version at all, or even Tyndale's for that matter. As indicated previously, even the first editions of the King James Version would be difficult for the modern reader.

It has been the goal of modern translators to present the Word of God in English that is clearly understood rather than in words and phrases that have lost their meaning to modern man.

Archaic and Obsolete Words

When the King James Version appeared in 1611, it utilized the English in common use at that time—the language spoken by people in everyday life. No one doubts that the translators did a superb job in capturing literary beauty as they translated God's Word into Elizabethan English.

However, Elizabethan English is not the common language of people today. The English of the King James Version is not *koine* (common) English today as was the Greek of the New Testament when originally written. Any piece of literature that is nearly four centuries old is bound to have expressions that are archaic and obsolete. Because the English language has gone through tremendous change and growth, it has been affected by time even more than other languages might be.

The following are some instances of words used

in the King James Version that are no longer in current usage and are thus not immediately understandable to the present generation:

Exodus 9:31: "The flax was *bolled.*"
"Bolled" is an old word for "podded" or "in bloom."

Exodus 28:8: "The *curious* girdle of the ephod."
"Curious" meant "artful" or "skillful."

Exodus 28:11,13,14: "*ouches.*"
This word meant "brooches" or "settings."

Deuteronomy 21:4: "A rough valley, which is neither *eared* nor sown."
"Eared" is an old word meaning "plowed."

Deuteronomy 28:26: "No man shall *fray* them away."
The word "fray" meant "scare."

Judges 9:53: "All to brake his skull."
This is an old phrase meaning "entirely broke his skull."

Judges 18:21: "The *carriage* before them."
"Carriage" meant "baggage."

II Samuel 14:26: "He *polled* his head."
This is an old phrase meaning "trimmed, or cut, his hair."

Job 9:33: "Neither is there any *daysman.*"
"Daysman" is an old word for "mediator" or "arbitrator."

Job 41:18: "His *neesings.*"
"Neesing" is an old word referring to "sneezing."

Psalm 35:15: "The *abjects* gathered themselves together against me."
"Abjects" is an old word for "slanderer" or "smiter."

Isaiah 3:18: "The Lord will take away the *bravery* of their tinkling ornaments."

"Bravery" meant "finery."

Isaiah 8:21: "Hardly *bestead* and hungry."

"Bestead" meant "situated."

Jeremiah 46:4: "Put on the *brigandines.*"

The word "brigandines" referred to "coats of armor."

Joel 2:24: "The *fats* shall overflow."

"Fats" is an old word for "vats."

Matthew 13:21: "By and by."

This phrase meant "immediately" or "shortly."

Matthew 14:11: "Was brought in a *charger.*"

The word "charger" referred to a "platter."

I Peter 3:11: "Let him *eschew* evil."

The word "eschew" meant "turn away" or "shun."

In addition to these specific examples, there are also other words in the King James Version that are not meaningful today, such as "charity" for "love," "entreat" for "treat," "conversation" for "conduct" or "manner of life," "convince" for "convict," "prevent" for "precede," "quick" for "alive," "quicken" for "revive," "script" for "small bag" or "wallet," "careful" for "anxious" or "worried," "sith" for "since," "do you to wit" for "cause you to know," "dispensation" for "stewardship," "trow" for "trust," "ghost" for "spirit."

These words were excellent choices when the King James Version was produced in 1611 because they were commonly used in everyday life. But time has changed the English language, so changes are necessary in translation work if there is to be proper communication. For instance, the word

53

"nephew" in 1611 meant "grandchild" or "descendant." Because the word now has a different meaning it is important for a translation to reflect that if a verse such as I Timothy 5:4, which mentions nephews, is to be properly understood.

More and Older Manuscripts

Another key reason for recent translations is the fact that, since 1611 when the King James Version was produced, additional and older manuscripts of the Bible in the original languages have been discovered. These manuscripts throw additional light on the text which needs to be considered in translation work. With the exception of a few dissidents, biblical scholars maintain that we now have a purer text as a result of manuscript discoveries. This means that by a careful comparison of the variant readings it is now possible to construct a text which is much closer to what the inspired authors actually wrote.

The oldest New Testament manuscripts available to the King James translators were written at least 700 years after the time of Christ. But now complete manuscripts of the entire Bible dating back to around 300 years after the time of Christ are available. There are even some New Testament fragments that were written as early as 100 years after Christ's ascension; that is, about 25 or 30 years after the last book of the New Testament was written. As to the age of the copies of the Greek New Testament or parts of it, Dr. R. Laird Harris states: "A dozen or more are over 1,500 years old" (*Your Bible*, p. 51).

The oldest Old Testament manuscripts available in 1611 were produced about 800 years after the time of Christ. But some portions of the Old Testament dating back to 200 years *before* the time of Christ are now available. <u>In other words, these manuscripts are a thousand years older and closer to the original writings than the ones available in 1611 when the King James Version was translated.</u>

During the past 100 years the world's greatest Christian Bible scholars and linguists have diligently compared the many available Bible manuscripts, both later and older ones. These scholars believe they have arrived at a biblical text that is more than 99 percent pure in relation to the original writings.

Translators of modern English versions have made use of the knowledge gained through the study of more manuscripts. An example is the New American Standard Bible. When the New Testament was published in 1963, the preface stated: "In revising the ASV [American Standard Version], consideration was given to the latest available manuscripts with a view to determining the best Greek text." Concerning modern English usage, the same preface stated: "The attempt has been made to render the grammar and terminology of the ASV in contemporary English. When it was felt that the word-for-word literalness of the ASV was unacceptable to the modern reader, a change was made in the direction of a more current English idiom."

Concerning the New American Standard Bible, the late Dr. Wilbur M. Smith stated, "In my opinion this is certainly the most accurate and the most revealing translation . . . that we now have. I intend to keep it on my desk for immediate access" (cited in *What Bible Can You Trust?* p. 79).

Omissions in Newer Versions

A criticism that has often been leveled against the modern English versions is that certain words or passages are omitted from the text. The implication of such a charge is that the translators had the subtle purpose of changing the Bible, particularly in passages dealing with the Person of Christ. So it is logical to ask, What is the reason for these omissions?

The commonly cited omissions in the modern English versions often involve words, phrases or passages that appear in the King James Version but are left out in other versions. Most of the contemporary English versions have not been revisions of the King James Version, which is itself only a translation, although it is a good one. Those working on the modern English versions have gone back beyond any translation to the Hebrew and Greek manuscripts. The omissions that are sometimes noticed when comparing these modern versions to the King James Version occur because the particular words or phrases in question are regarded as not having validity in the original writings. Where the translators feel assured, on the basis of manuscript studies, that a passage does not belong in the Scriptures, it is omitted. If the authenticity of a passage is questioned, it may be included in the margin with an indication of its doubtful status, or it may be embraced in the text, either in italicized print or in brackets. Marginal notes often indicate the reason for the questionable validity of the words at issue.

Since most people do not have the ability to study the biblical manuscripts, they may question the reasoning and decisions of the translators. However, sound biblical scholars should be credited with sincerity and integrity, not with evil motives. The majority of Bible translations have been produced by earnest, godly and evangelical scholars. Although some translations have been produced by committees which included non-evangelical scholars, only evangelicals were involved in producing the Amplified Bible, the Berkeley Version, the New American Standard Bible and the New International Version, to name a few.

Colossians 1:14

The significant differences in these modern versions from the King James Version are due mainly to variations between the presently accepted Greek text and the older Textus Receptus, discussed previously. A passage frequently referred to by opponents of modern versions is the first phrase of Colossians 1:14. The King James Version reads: "In whom we have redemption through his blood." Virtually all other English versions simply read: "In whom we have redemption," omitting "through his blood."

Some sincere people conclude from this comparison that the translators of modern English versions were attempting to do away with the blood atonement of Jesus Christ. A check through the King James New Testament indicates that the blood of Christ is mentioned 33 times. A check through the New International Version, for instance, indicates that in every instance the words "the blood" are retained, except in Colossians 1:14. If the translators were deliberately attempting to eliminate the idea of blood atonement, they would certainly have left out the word in more than one of the 33 instances.

Why then is the phrase "through his blood" in Colossians 1:14 omitted in the modern English versions? It is because the translators of those versions do not believe there is proper manuscript authority for assuming that this phrase appeared in the original letter Paul wrote to the Colossians. It would be difficult to find a New Testament scholar, evangelical or otherwise, who maintains that the phrase "through his blood" is part of the original text of Colossians 1:14. Even the late, highly esteemed gospel preacher and Bible scholar Dr. Harry A. Ironside stated in his commentary on Colossians: "There is some question as to the MS. [manuscript] authority of the expression, 'through His blood.' The best editors generally omit it" (*Lectures on Colossians*, p. 40). J. N. Darby, who is attributed with originating the so-called Plymouth Brethren movement, omits "through his blood" from Colossians 1:14 in his translation of the Scriptures. Darby most certainly was a staunch fundamentalist.

This particular passage is cited merely to illustrate why certain "omissions," based on textual grounds, occur in the modern English versions. Regardless of whether or not the translators have always been correct in determining the purest Greek text, their motives should not be condemned nor should they be considered enemies and deliberate corrupters of the Scriptures. It is one thing to disagree with a biblical scholar, but it is quite another thing to count him as an enemy of the Word of God because he does not agree with the opinions of others, which are usually based on much less knowledge and information.

There have been, of course, agnostic and skeptical biblical scholars who have not accepted the Bible as God's Word, yet who have sought to protect themselves under the umbrella of "scholarship." Earlier theologically liberal scholars did much to undermine faith in the Word of God, and their modern successors are pursuing the same tactics. But these are not the people who have produced the translations of the Bible in current English language. It would be highly improbable that any person who is determined to destroy the Bible would spend years of his life in a painstaking effort to put it into contemporary language, making it more understandable and more appealing to the masses in today's world.

The Aim: Better Translation

Another reason for the modern versions of the Bible has been the desire to produce a better translation. Archaeological findings and extensive scholarship in the *koine* Greek of the New Testament have thrown new light on many passages of Scripture. This has helped to give more correct renderings of certain words and phrases. This new light has contributed not only toward clearer translations but also toward the production of numerous valuable biblical commentaries and other works.

59

Many people in the English world have revered the King James Version as being a virtually perfect translation, whereas this is obviously not the case. No translation is perfect. Only the original writings were inspired of God; therefore, only the original writings were inerrant, or without error.

Not to discredit the remarkable King James Version but to demonstrate why later translations have been made, note the following examples. In I Samuel 10:24, and in seven other instances in the Old Testament, the expression "God save the king" occurs. However, the word "God" does not occur in this phrase in any Hebrew text. The Hebrew text simply reads, "Live the king!" "God save the king" was a phrase used by Englishmen as an expression of goodwill toward their monarchs. Because this was a common expression in the time of King James, and since the translators obviously held deep respect for their monarch, they put this in the translation without any textual warrant.

In chapters 3, 11 and 12 of the Book of Exodus, the King James Version states that the people of Israel "borrowed" objects of wealth from the Egyptians at the command of God as they were leaving Egypt. Yet it is clear from the context that the Israelites had no intention of returning what they "borrowed." Critics of the Bible have made a strong issue of this, terming it dishonesty and deceit under the claim of divine sanction. However, the word translated "borrow" means "to ask." According to the authoritative commentary on the Old Testament by Keil and Delitzsch, this word conveyed not only the idea of simple asking but also of demanding what was rightly owed. Obviously, God would not command a person to "borrow" something from his neighbor and then steal out of the country without returning what was borrowed. The newer versions correct this translation by using the words "ask" or "request."

The word "candlestick" is used repeatedly in the King James Version, but today something different is understood by this term. Candles, as they are known today, did not exist in Bible times. Lamps with wicks, fueled by olive oil, were used then. The Hebrew word should more understandably be translated "lampstand" instead of "candlestick."

There are also New Testament examples. In the expression "God forbid," which occurs 14 times in the New Testament, the word "God" is not in the original text in a single instance. In a sense, the King James translators were paraphrasing in order to use an expression of their time to help communicate what was meant by the Greek words. The expression should more literally be translated "Let it not be!"

Another example is the use of the word "bishop" in I Timothy 3:1,2. The Greek word involved means "overseer." However, at the time the King James Version was being produced, an overseer in the Church of England was known as a "bishop." Therefore, this word was used by the translators. Something quite different is understood by the word "bishop" today, however.

As previously indicated, these cases are not cited to undermine a great, long-enduring translation of the Bible, but simply to show why later translations have been produced. They are made in an effort to improve on an already basically good translation. Whatever degree of success modern translators have or have not achieved, the purpose of most of them has been to produce a clearer and more understandable version of the Bible, based on the Greek and Hebrew texts. As mentioned, these texts are believed to be at least 99 percent pure; that is, as the writings actually were when first written.

Chapter 5

The Present Enigma

Generally speaking, English versions of the Bible can be grouped into three categories—translations, free translations and paraphrases.

Kinds of English Versions

A translation endeavors, as much as possible, to translate verbatim, or word for word, what is in the Hebrew and Greek texts, adding only what is necessary to make the expression understood in the other language. The King James Version fits into this category, as do such modern English versions as the New American Standard Bible and the New International Version.

A free, or expanded, translation also deals with the specific words involved, but it endeavors to bring out the fine shades of meaning of the original languages by expanding the translation for the English reader. Sometimes this tends to overtranslation, and the end result may not really be in the language commonly used by the reader. Examples of free translations are The New Testament, by Charles B. Williams; Expanded Translation of the Greek New Testament, by Kenneth S. Wuest; and The Amplified Bible.

A paraphrase, on the other hand, is not concerned with carrying over the meaning of the exact words of Scripture. Rather, it restates the text by giving the meaning in another form. Examples of paraphrases are the Living Bible, produced by Kenneth Taylor, and The New Testament in Modern English, by J. B. Phillips.

A paraphrase of the Bible, in its best sense, is produced through the study of the Hebrew and Greek texts, plus a comparison of existing translations. Then the understood sense is restated in the words of the person, or persons, doing the paraphrasing. A paraphrase, therefore, is a sort of commentary because it embodies the interpretation and theological views of those who did the work.

Paraphrases can be helpful for personal reading, and the renderings are often refreshing, but they should not be regarded as precise translations, which are produced to communicate the meaning of the actual words in the Hebrew and Greek testaments, adding only what is required to make it understandable in another language.

As a general rule, paraphrases—and for that matter translations—are more reliable when they have been produced by a group of scholars rather than primarily by a single individual.

Most Christians desire their Bible to be in dignified and reverent language which is becoming to the Word of God. While the language must be common and readily understandable, it should never be slangy or vulgar. Some of the private translations of today, in my opinion, have expressions that are on the verge of slang.

Current Difficulties

There are so many English versions of the Bible

in common use today that confusion often results. A Christian often does not know which version will be used by others in public reading and teaching. As a result, understanding and blessing is hindered because of the difficulty of following in a different translation. Public reading of the Scriptures in worship, alternately or in unison, is difficult, or even impossible, because of the various versions now in common use. For the sake of effective communication it would seem wise for a local church to agree, as much as possible, on the version that will be commonly used in its services.

Which version to use in memorizing scripture also presents a problem. Most adults over 40 years of age have memorized from the King James Version and find it extremely difficult to memorize from another. However, others who have not memorized extensively from the King James Version would not find it as difficult to memorize from another.

In the days of King James I a solution was relatively simple. Although several versions had been in common use in the churches and among the clergymen for several years, the king—as head of the Church of England—could officially order the making of a new version. But no parallel to the situation of that time exists today. There is no official state religion with an authoritative voice concerning the Scriptures or a creed pertaining to the Scriptures. Although a particular denomination or a Christian organization might recommend a particular version of the Bible to its constituents, it cannot demand that the recommended version be the sole translation of its adherents. Hence, the picture of the future is not clear.

Names of Reliable Versions

Amid the confusion about Bible translations and versions, Christian leaders are invariably asked, "Which of the modern versions are reliable?" or "Which translation do you recommend?" In response to such queries I usually single out three of the contemporary versions. The New Berkeley Version, published in 1969 by Zondervan, is a worthy translation of the entire Bible, true to the original languages and written in modern English. It is the product of reputable evangelical scholars who are committed to the conviction of plenary inspiration, and it has been recommended by such known Christian scholars as E. Schuyler English and W. A. Criswell and by the late Donald Grey Barnhouse and V. Raymond Edman.

The New American Standard Bible is another well accepted translation. Although it is based on the principles used in the American Standard Version of 1901, it is actually a new translation rather than a mere revision. This translation is also the product of sound evangelical scholarship. It is an excellent translation from the original languages, although the "flow" of the English is not as smooth as in some versions.

A third version which I personally like and esteem is the New International Version. It is the work of a large group of men of impeccable scholarship and positive evangelical conviction who represent several Christian organizations. Not only is it an excellent translation of the original Scriptures, but its English has the two unique characteristics of dignity and simplicity—dignity that befits the Word of God, and simplicity for a greater understanding of that Word.

The picture for the future of English translations is not clear. Whether there will be this continued confusion or whether a single new translation will rise to the top as the commonly used Bible cannot really be predicted. One can only hope that God, in His sovereignty, will cause the best translation to rise to the top and less worthy ones to be dropped by the wayside, as has happened in the past. Meanwhile, it is to be hoped that discerning Christians will not use unworthy versions or paraphrases simply because they are so easy to read.

If what I have said in this book helps English-speaking Christians to understand the background of translations and to choose the best of the modern versions, I will be deeply grateful.